FABIAN SOCIETY

D1800130

The Fabian Society is Britain's leading left of centre think tank and political society, committed to creating the political ideas and policy debates which can shape the future of progressive politics.

With over 300 Fabian MPs, MEPs, Peers, MSPs and AMs, the Society plays an unparalleled role in linking the ability to influence policy debates at the highest level with vigorous grassroots debate among our growing membership of over 7000 people, 70 local branches meeting regularly throughout Britain and a vibrant Young Fabian section organising its own activities. Fabian publications, events and ideas therefore reach and influence a wider audience than those of any comparable think tank. The Society is unique among think tanks in being a thriving, democratically-constituted membership organisation, affiliated to the Labour Party but organisationally and editorially independent.

For over 120 years Fabians have been central to every important renewal and revision of left of centre thinking. The Fabian commitment to open and participatory debate is as important today as ever before as we explore the ideas, politics and policies which will define the next generation of progressive politics in Britain, Europe and around the world.

Fabian Society
11 Dartmouth Street
London SW1H 9BN
www.fabians.org.uk

Fabian Policy Report 63

First published 2010
ISBN 978 0 7163 3063 9

Editorial Director: Tom Hampson
Editorial Manager: Ed Wallis

To find out more about the Fabian Society, the Young
Fabians, the Fabian Women's Network and our local
societies, please visit our web site at **www.fabians.org.uk**.

Hardest to Reach?

The politics of multiple needs and exclusions

Edited by Tom Hampson

Project partners

About the Calouste Gulbenkian Foundation

The Calouste Gulbenkian Foundation's purpose in the UK and Ireland is to help enrich and connect the experiences of individuals and secure lasting and beneficial change. It has a special interest in supporting those who are most disadvantaged. The Foundation was established in Lisbon in 1956. The UK Branch, based in London, has for more than 50 years initiated and supported pioneering cultural, social and educational developments. www.gulbenkian.org.uk

About the Making Every Adult Matter coalition

Making Every Adult Matter (MEAM) is a coalition of four national charities – Clinks, DrugScope, Homeless Link and Mind – formed to influence policy and services for adults with multiple needs and exclusions. Together, the charities represent over 1600 frontline organisations working in the criminal justice, drug treatment, homelessness and mental health sectors. The coalition is supported by the Calouste Gulbenkian Foundation.

About the authors

Hilary Armstrong is the Labour MP for North West Durham. She served as Minister for Local Government, Minister for Social Exclusion and Labour Chief Whip.

Iain Duncan Smith is the Conservative MP for Chingford and Wood Green and Chair of the Centre for Social Justice.

David Halpern is Director of Research at the Institute for Government, having previously worked as Chief Analyst in the Prime Minister's Strategy Unit.

Tom Hampson is Editorial Director at the Fabian Society, having previously worked at Hobsbawm Macaulay and the think tank Demos.

Oliver Hilbery is Project Director for the Making Every Adult Matter coalition.

Peter Kellner is President of the polling organisation YouGov and a journalist and political commentator.

Alasdair Murray is Director of CentreForum, the independent liberal think tank.

Akash Paun is a Senior Researcher at the Institute for Government.

CONTENTS

INTRODUCTION: REAL LIVES

Tom Hampson and Oliver Hilbery

"I just want to be happy and feel part of this world, not an outsider."[1]

In 2010 there remains a small group of people, spread through every community in Britain, who are living deeply chaotic lives. These individuals share our communities, our aspirations and our own daily lives. Yet they are often homeless, sleeping rough on our streets or serving short-term prison sentences. Many are trapped in a spiral of drugs, mental ill health and crime. All are 'recycling' between service interventions without ever getting the coordinated help they need. And as the recession continues to bite, this disjointed approach is costing an awful lot in terms of money and wasted potential.

Since 1997 the Government has often claimed the high ground in tackling exclusion. We have witnessed the setting up of the Social Exclusion Unit and Task Force, the creation of a dedicated Social Exclusion Minister and direct prime ministerial engagement. And there has indeed been some considerable success in tackling wider social exclusion. Child poverty has fallen, the number of people sleeping rough has fallen dramatically, and public services across education, health and social care have seen increases in funding and improving results.

But many people across the political spectrum will look at this small yet highly visible group of people who are routinely excluded and living chaotic lives and they will feel that politics has failed. The public too are taking notice. As new attitudes work for this book shows, far from being hostile they remain optimistic about the hidden potential of these individuals and for society's role in helping them achieve better lives.

Fortunately, many of the political and practical solutions that can improve the lives of people facing multiple needs and exclusions are now understood. Yet overall implementation remains patchy, responsibility for action is often offloaded and as a country we still seem unable to fully tackle the problem.

It is now time to build on our learning and to move forward. We need a cross-party consensus for action and a multiple needs Green Paper early in the next parliament to set out the government's vision and approach. Locally we must accept the case for action and strengthen implementation of the services that work. As Iain Duncan Smith, Hilary Armstrong and Alasdair Murray show in Chapters 2, 3 and 4, the policies and ideas are there. This group of people can and should be included in our vision of a just and fair society.

"I would like to have a flat I can keep, be able to look out for myself, something to do that help others and a life free of stress and bad people."

Who? Chaotic lives that are costly to society

Individuals with multiple needs and exclusions are a small subset of the two to three per cent of the population who suffer from 'deep and persistent exclusion'.[2] As well as facing multiple needs – such as homelessness, substance misuse, mental ill health and offending – this group are also routinely excluded from effective contact with the services they need and tend to live chaotic lives that are costly to society. National estimates, made difficult by a lack of data, converge on around 56,000 individuals at any one time, found mainly in the homelessness or prison population. Locally, the picture is much clearer. Individuals with multiple needs are often very well-known to a wide range of local services – indeed in many areas a handful of individuals are so ubiquitous that they are known by name among local authority directors, health teams, the police and voluntary services.

What? Services that exclude
For those affected, facing multiple needs is just part of the problem. The real difficulties arise when they try and seek help from a range of services that are designed to deal with one problem at a time. When that predictably fails to work, they are excluded, or exclude themselves, as services and agencies compete to avoid responsibility. The situation is particularly difficult for individuals who have no 'main' need but a multitude of lower-level problems which together are a serious cause for concern.

"With some people if you've got either drugs or mental health problems they are willing to help you, but if you have both they're like 'oh they've brought on their mental health problems themselves.'"

"It's like one part doesn't know what the other part's doing. You can talk to someone and then see somebody else the next time and they don't even know that you have actually spoke to somebody before."

"People don't know what it's like unless they've actually done it themselves. I mean I've been in situations where I wanted to give up…and I didn't know where to turn to. There was nobody there to say 'oh we can help you do this' or 'we can help you do that'"

As a result, many individuals start to use expensive emergency interventions – police, ambulances and A&E – as their first port of call rather than as a final resort. Of course many also fall into the one service that won't exclude them – the criminal justice system. Yet even here, or on release, they fail to receive the coordinated help they need.

"I was going into prison, I was serving my time in there and then I found myself being released and just going back into the community and I'd be alright for a week or so and then I'd find myself start drifting again, and not really knowing where to turn to."

"No one is saying anything [about] where you can get help. You have to go and look for it and I think there should be more awareness in jail and when you get out of where the help is and where you can get help."

"There was one time where I actually went out and got myself arrested on purpose because I didn't know what to do, where to turn to, so I actually used the police, if you like, and custody, as somewhere to go, someone to turn to and then using prison as somewhere to live, as I had no other option, if you like, apart from being homeless, which is, you know, something I didn't really want to do."

For the taxpayer, the financial costs can be shockingly high. One indivual, a former drug addict and serial offender, was estimated to have cost government more than £400,000 over several years in direct costs alone.[3] This money is spent in a disconnected, unplanned way and too often supports individuals to remain in difficult circumstances rather than move forward with their lives.

How have we got here? Why do people – especially those costing the taxpayer the most – often continue to fall between the gaps?

Part of the answer, as David Halpern and Akash Paun argue in Chapter 5, is that both national policy and what happens on the ground often fail to be joined up. On the one hand, a range of different cultures and systems operate across Whitehall and amongst civil servants and policy makers, with budgets split across government departments, a narrow focus on departmental concerns, little collective decision making and no clear ownership of the problem.

Meanwhile at the local level, as outlined above, agencies are often bad at communicating with each other and everyone avoids responsibility. Inflexible cultures, targets, budgets, staff attitudes, strict eligibility criteria and a lack of suitable assessment lead to this group being ineffectively served. Partly this is the fault of national policy drivers and a lack of joined up commissioning, but local statutory partners and the voluntary sector too must work harder to remove the silos in their delivery – something that the Making Every Adult Matter coalition is committed to achieving.

Towards the solutions

Fortunately a way forward is beginning to emerge. Both policy and practice have come a long way in recent years.

In 2006 the Social Exclusion Task Force published *Reaching Out*, an action plan on social exclusion. For the first time it explicitly recognised adults with multiple needs and exclusions, the barriers they face to service delivery and the government's overarching vision of "public services that identify and persistently support people with chaotic lives and multiple needs".

This was followed in 2007 by PSA 16, the top level cross-government target on social exclusion which has made headway around focusing local activity on people with complex needs. Recently, too, a number of government strategies have made specific mention of multiple needs and exclusions and the solutions required. However, the issue of multiple needs and exclusions is still far from being uniformly recognised across government and despite its good progress PSA 16 focuses by definition on four groups of people who are already well linked to services.

On the ground, too, we are now much clearer about what works for this group. The Adults Facing Chronic Exclusion (ACE) Programme, launched as part of the *Reaching Out* action plan, above, has tested a range of service interventions and taught us much about the key aspects of service delivery required for this group. Often the solutions are simpler than one might expect. We have learnt that multiple needs services can coordinate access to other services and provide the 'consistent, trusted adult' so often missing in people's lives; that they work best when they have full strategic and political support in local areas; and that it is essential for 'mainstream' services to be willing to 'flex' their eligibility criteria or 'go the extra mile' to ensure that they respond for an individual rather than shirking responsibility. These findings have been echoed by other work in local areas over the years in particular from Revolving Doors and specialist local multiple needs teams such as the Elmore Team in Oxford. Individuals facing multiple needs often say that an interaction with a service that focuses on multiple needs is the first time they have felt listened to and valued for a long time:

"There was also a referral system, or signposting if you like, where they'd speak to me, see what was going on and then say ok I think these people might [help]… and this was the first time that this had actually happened to me. I started to feel a little bit valued, like someone was actually listening to what was going on. I wasn't thinking I was going to end up homeless again."

"I was given a key worker, and I built up some really good rapport with this lady... She started to come to appointments with me, come

to the council, help me fill out forms that I needed to, for the accommodation…So that started to work for me."

"They've been absolutely brilliant actually, I was there yesterday. I was speaking to my key worker and she's helping me with my mental problems, she's helping with my drugs problems, she's helping me find some place to live and I'm working with another woman from [the service] who is helping me to get back into work."

"Fifteen years I was on-and-off taking heroin, been to jail several times, I've spent most of my life in jail, suffering from mental problems…Finally I found [the service]…[now] I haven't committed no crimes. I've sorted a lot of my mental problems out; I don't take drugs anymore."

"Their staff have listened to me and treated me as a human being and not a machine that has broken down and needed repair. These services have opened doors for me and given me good information and support."

Making it happen

Yet even though the local solutions are perhaps relatively simple and policy across government is beginning to develop, there remains a massive challenge and lack of implementation – partly because local areas still struggle to recognise the benefits and partly because government is yet to make it a political priority.

A stronger national focus on multiple needs and exclusions is needed to encourage activity in local areas. This need not be prescriptive about local delivery, nor does it need to define the group from the 'top down,' but it should ensure that every area has considered multiple needs and exclusions, knows who its small group of people are and has a plan in place to address their needs.

In this time of economic constraint government must make the case that any area ignoring this group is wasting its resources, even if this can't be seen in local budget sheets, which tend to only show parts of the picture. And if that is not enough it can also suggest how a focus on multiple needs and exclusions will benefit a whole range of shared social policy objectives, from ending rough sleeping to reducing reoffending.

The Making Every Adult Matter coalition is calling for the next Government, of whatever composition, to lay out its thinking on achieving this focus in a multiple needs Green Paper early in the next parliament.

Some may argue that there is a lack of political will – a hesitancy to focus coherently on a group of people who are seen as so marginalised. But as Peter Kellner outlines in the opening chapter of this book, politicians should not be afraid of public opinion on this issue. Voters are concerned about people with multiple needs and exclusions, they value their potential and can see the benefits of intervening – both social and economic. They will not stand in the way of action.

It is time to be honest about the political and practical challenges and the good reasons for overcoming them. Helping this group of people is key to social justice, public service reform and many other policy areas. But getting it right will also be good for British politics and ultimately good for everyone.

Footnotes

1 Thank are due to members of the Revolving Doors National Service User Forum for all the quotes used in this chapter. See http://www.revolving-doors.org.uk for more information.

2 This figure is from Cabinet Office, 2007. Reaching Out: Progress on Social Exclusion, p.5

3 Source: Making Every Adult Matter, 2009. Four Point Manifesto, p22.

1. YES, IF...

Peter Kellner

While politicians have sometimes shied away from tackling the most entrenched issues around people with multiple needs, new YouGov polling – conducted for this book – shows that the public are very concerned about this group and think government has a responsibility to make a difference. Politicians should stop being nervous of public opinion – and embrace people's desire for real change.

Should we – society, taxpayers, government – do more to help people with multiple needs? At a time when pressure on public spending is likely to be acute for some years (whoever is in power at Westminster) can a case be made for increasing support for those affected by a combination of problems such as homelessness, mental ill-health, offending, drug addiction and alcoholism?

Our new data suggests that the answer is "yes"; or, rather, "yes, if". Most of the public believe that better services for people with multiple needs can be regarded as a form of investment: more coordinated services now would save money later on or help individuals contribute more to society. Government interventions presented in this way would receive good levels of public support.

First, we set out the meaning of 'multiple needs and exclusions' and how men and women affected by them "often end up sleeping rough or 'recycling' between prison and the community". Two-thirds of the public say they are personally

Table 1: Public concern

Q: How concerned are you personally about the problems of such people (with multiple needs and exclusions)?

Very concerned	21
Fairly concerned	47
TOTAL CONCERNED	**68**
Not very concerned	24
Not at all concerned	4
TOTAL NOT CONCERNED	**28**
Don't know	4

Table 2: Society

Q: And how concerned do you think society generally should be about the problems of such people?

Very concerned	37
Fairly concerned	48
TOTAL CONCERNED	**85**
Not very concerned	9
Not at all concerned	2
TOTAL NOT CONCERNED	**11**
Don't know	4

concerned about people with such problems. Perhaps a more relevant number is the 21 per cent who say they are "very concerned": this is probably a better measure of real public concern. So while it is not a majority passion there are significant levels of concern from the public for individuals in this group.

When asked how concerned "society generally" should be, the total saying "very" or "fairly" concerned jumps to 85 per cent, with 37 per cent saying "very concerned" – again, a minority but, this time, a rather larger minority.

So public concern exists, but it would still be relatively easy for any government to ignore the issue and hope it will go away, which, of course, it won't. Suppose ministers and other politicians took a long view and decided that for social and economic reasons they must act. At a time when every penny of public spending must be justified, could they persuade the electorate of the case for giving a priority to the task of tackling multiple needs?

YouGov's poll suggests that they could. While the public are hardly clamouring for action (indeed, we usually find that when they are asked to identify the main cause of problems faced by the most marginalised, they blame a mix of factors and sometimes the people themselves) it is also clear they won't stand in the way of change. They can see what the benefits of action would be. Six out of ten electors agree that if the government and local services did more to help people with multiple needs and exclusions "the individuals would be able to contribute more to society". By more than six-to-one they outnumber those who say "I do not think any benefits would result". It is widely thought that society would benefit in a number of other ways too: the people themselves would be able to contribute more (58 per cent), fewer crimes would be committed (50 per cent), local communities would be stronger (32 per cent) and the cycle of despair would be broken, with fewer people in the future facing multiple needs and exclusions (40 per cent). These figures show a snapshot of public opinion as it currently stands – in the absence of any sustained local or national government initiative to tackle these problems. Were such an initiative to be launched, the numbers anticipating a positive impact would be expected to rise.

It is interesting that 'future contribution' tops the table of perceived benefits of action, for we know that this is also what often drives sympathy towards this group. Previous

Table 3: Results

Q: If the Government and local services did more to help people with multiple needs and exclusions which, if any, of the following benefits do you think would result? (Please tick all that apply.)

The individuals would be able to contribute more to society	58
Fewer crimes would be committed	50
The government would save money in the future	41
It would reduce the number of people facing multiple needs and exclusions in the future	40
It would be fairer on those people more likely to suffer from multiple needs and exclusions	35
Local communities would be stronger	32
Other	1
Not applicable - I do not think any benefits would result	9
Don't know	11

work by YouGov for the Fabian Society found that a belief that those receiving help would go on to contribute more to society in the future was the single biggest factor in influencing support for welfare. It was a much more powerful driver of attitudes to welfare than beliefs about how people got into

Table 4: Sympathy

Q: Which, if any, do you think would make you MORE sympathetic towards their situation? (Please tick all the examples below that would make you MORE sympathetic.)

If they had looked for help and not found it	63
If they were motivated to improve their situation	58
If they had poor mental wellbeing	54
If they had suffered abuse in childhood	47
If they could not rely on friends or family	37
If they faced significant barriers to employment	33
If the difficulties they faced were similar to the difficulties faced by other people you know	21
That if they were dependent on drugs or alcohol it was because of other issues in their lives	16
That if they committed crime it was because of other issues in their lives	11
Not applicable - none of these would make me more sympathetic towards their situation	8
Don't know	8

difficulties in the first place. People can be prepared to forgive past behaviour if someone is genuinely trying now.

And key here was an individual's intentions; not how much they could put back into society, but that they were prepared to try.

So it is no surprise that the factors that our latest polling finds most effective for increasing sympathy towards those with multiple needs are beliefs that the person is 'motivated to improve their situation' or concrete demonstration of good intentions ('if they had looked for help and not found it'). Demonstrating that those receiving help are taking it in good faith and showing that people do go on to contribute to society in whatever way they find possible can therefore be a powerful driver of public support for assistance.

There is also a strong view that government and local services currently have a disjointed approach for this group and that a stronger focus would help improve situations for people with multiple needs and exclusions (Tables 6 and 7).

Overall, it is clear that voters are far more likely to welcome than resist any plans to address multiple needs and exclusions more ambitiously.

Table 5: Contribution

Q: Which of these statements comes closest to your view?	
If people with multiple needs and exclusions are given help to improve their lives, they will be able to contribute much more to society in the future	59
People with multiple needs and exclusions – even when given help – will always end up back in the same situation eventually	26
Don't know	15

Table 6: Disjointed government

Q: From what you know, do you think...

Government and local services have a disjointed service response for people with multiple needs and exclusions	66
Government and local services already work fairly well together to provide a service for people with multiple needs and exclusions	15
Don't know	19

Table 7: Stronger focus

If government and local services had a stronger focus on people with multiple needs and exclusions and worked better for them, do you think...?

It would help improve the situation of this group	63
It wouldn't make any difference to the situation of this group	21
Don't know	16

Table 8: Politicians

Q: Do you think...?

Politicians can make a difference to the lives of people with multiple needs and exclusions	52
There is not much that politicians can do to change the lives of people with multiple needs and exclusions	34
Don't know	14

Hardest to Reach?

2. MULTIPLE SOLUTIONS

Iain Duncan Smith

If we are to truly transform the lives of people experiencing multiple needs and exclusions then a radically different model is needed; for too long this group has been left behind. We must start seeing people as individuals and, rather than delivering services in silos, take a holistic approach to addressing their often complex needs. Sustainable reform demands a preventative, evidence-led approach with truly multi-agency working.

As Chairman of the Centre for Social Justice I have spent a great deal of time visiting voluntary sector projects that work with individuals who have lived their lives at the very margins of society. I have spoken with addicts who have spent years cycling between life on the streets and in prison, committing crime to fund their habit. I have visited homeless projects whose clients have suffered mental and physical health problems, both cause and consequence of years of alcohol and drug abuse. These are often people who grew up in chaotic and dysfunctional families, who fell out of the education system at an early age and who, ultimately, felt entirely rejected by society.

It was to champion the plight of those facing such profound needs that I founded the Centre for Social Justice. The CSJ exists, quite simply, to put social justice at the heart of British politics. We seek to understand the drivers behind poverty and social exclusion and to recommend effective policy solutions to them.

Over the past decades, social breakdown has become increasingly entrenched in our most deprived communities. Whilst the Government has been focused on poverty as a whole, it has all but ignored those living in severe, often persistent, poverty. The arbitrary poverty line – at 60 per cent of median income – has created a perverse target: there may be fewer people living in poverty now than in 1997, but our analysis of poverty trends revealed more people living in *severe* poverty.[1] Despite billions of pounds of investment in government initiatives such as the New Deals, Sure Start, NOMs and drug treatment programmes, the lives of the very poorest in society have not improved. An incoming government must rectify this.

For too long the approach to poverty and social exclusion has been economic, but poverty is far more than just the absence of money. The CSJ has identified five key pathways to poverty – family breakdown, economic dependency, educational failure, addiction and personal indebtedness – and it is on these drivers that we must concentrate more of our efforts.

Crucially, where one driver is present, more often than not so too are the others. Debt, for example, is a key driver of family breakdown and family breakdown can lead to failed education which in turn can significantly reduce that child's future employment prospects, increasing their likelihood of offending and taking drugs.

It is therefore vital that politicians and policy-makers recognise that any attempt to tackle poverty must be multifaceted, something which has too often been missing. Implementing policies to address any one of the pathways in isolation will only ever have limited impact. The life of an individual facing multiple needs and exclusions will only be *sustainably* transformed with a holistic approach: unlike government departments and their attitudes to social issues, people do not live their lives in silos.

I believe that with a much more comprehensive approach, and one which looks at not just the programmes being delivered but the processes and structures within which delivery occurs, we really can bring those at the margins into the mainstream of society. Below is a five point approach for doing just that.

First, both national and local government should be doing much more to prevent negative outcomes in the first place. For the majority of homeless, addicted and offending adults their problems did not start in adulthood – the risk factors were evident much earlier.

If we are to transform the lives of those with multiple needs then a truly joined-up approach is needed.

Around half of all prisoners ran away from home as a child, almost a third were in local authority care, half were excluded from school and two thirds have a numeracy level below that of an 11 year old child.[2] Similarly, up to a third of rough sleepers were in care,[3] 40 per cent of homeless young women were sexually abused as children[4] and family conflict is the main immediate cause of homelessness for at least two thirds of homeless young people.[5] We also know that substance abuse correlates strongly with the experience of family breakdown and dysfunction amongst young people.[6]

In short, we know that growing up in a chaotic and fractured family environment is a key risk factor for future problems. It can condition the infant brain curtailing its development and reducing the child's life chances. Surely it would be better to get ahead of the curve and strengthen families rather than constantly trying to pick up the pieces after they have ceased to function?

The CSJ has looked extensively at the issue of early intervention – taking into account the most recent neuroscientific evidence – and we have made a number of key policy recommendations. These include enhancing the role of health visitors, building on Sure Start Children's Centres to create Family Hubs and rolling out proven intensive early intervention programmes such as the Nurse Family Partnership (NFP).[7] A comprehensive evaluation of the American NFP revealed significant benefits, ranging from a 79 per cent reduction in child maltreatment to an 81 per cent decline in convictions amongst adolescents.[8] These results speak for themselves. This is too important an issue to allow party politics to get in the way. I encourage politicians to follow the example that Graham Allen and I have set in co-authoring the report *Early Intervention* and work together to see this much needed agenda implemented.

Second, if we are to transform the lives of those with multiple needs then a truly joined-up approach is needed. Instead of funding individual departments to deliver programmes, funding should be attached to the delivery of policies which are *cross*-departmental. This would require buy-in from all relevant Secretaries of State via a co-ordinating body.[9] A similarly cross-departmental approach should be adopted at a local level. All programmes to do this should be overseen and coordinated by someone at cabinet level.

At a local level, much more effective sharing of data is needed. In our *Gangs* report we identified the failure of local agencies to highlight young people exhibiting risk factors until much too late, and recommended a new multi-agency model to overcome this.[10] The principle is the same for adults with multiple needs, and a similarly multi-agency model – one in which *all* relevant agencies, including local authorities, PCTs, police, housing and voluntary groups come together – should be applied.

Third, to maximise the effectiveness of this multi-agency approach local authorities should make use of the key worker model. As has been demonstrated in many of the Family Intervention Projects, providing a single point of reference for vulnerable and often chaotic individuals can be highly effective, and is less likely to mean people falling through cross-agency gaps.

Fourth, worklessness is one of the key drivers of poverty and is both cause and consequence of issues such as addiction, offending and homelessness. The prohibitively high participation and marginal tax rates currently embedded in the benefits system mean that, for many low income individuals, work simply does not pay. Rather than helping people out of poverty, the benefits system now has the perverse effect of trapping people in persistent unemployment. We should be encouraging people to make the transition into work, ensuring there are no barriers in the way of taking up work and – once they are there – using the voluntary sector, to support people to stay in work.

A socially and economically strong society is not one in which an entire section is left behind.

Our report *Dynamic Benefits* used dynamic modelling to produce a comprehensive blueprint for reforming the benefits system. This includes reducing effective tax rates by introducing one single withdrawal rate of 55 per cent (some groups currently lose up to 90 pence in every additional £1 earned), increasing the earnings disregard and simplifying the system.[11] Work is socially and financially

21

beneficial and is linked to better physical and mental health, we need a benefits system that reflects this.

Finally, national and local government should only be commissioning programmes that work. The current economic climate makes this imperative, but recession or no we should not be spending taxpayers' money on ineffective initiatives: the human as well as the financial cost to society is unacceptable. I have commissioned the CSJ to create a social return on investment (SROI) model for government. The private sector assesses the return on investment for different programmes aimed at achieving the same goals and uses the data to determine which programmes are adopted – government should do the same. Indeed, in the US, Washington Institute for Public Policy has been using an SROI model for years to determine how taxpayers' money is spent. We need a similar body in Britain to evaluate the impact of different programmes and ascertain their social and financial value. Not all addiction programmes, for example, or offender rehabilitation programmes are equal; far from it. Taxpayers deserve to know that their money is delivering real results, and those for which the money is being spent deserve a programme which will actually deliver life change.

For more than a decade government has been focused on alleviating poverty amongst those just below an arbitrary poverty threshold, this cannot continue. An incoming government must turn its attentions towards those who have been left to languish at the very margins of society, those in severe poverty. I believe that the reforms described above would transform the lives of society's most damaged individuals. But if doing the right thing is not reason enough for politicians, then let them remember that a socially and economically strong society is not one in which an entire section is left behind. The reforms detailed above will require political courage, but failure to demonstrate such courage is not just a wasted opportunity, it is an abdication of responsibility. Britain needs action now.

Footnotes

1 The Centre for Social Justice, December 2006, Breakdown Britain, Volume 1 Economic Dependency; severe poverty is measured as below 40% of median income
2 Social Exclusion Unit, 2002, Reducing Re-offending by ex-prisoners
3 Social Exclusion Unit, July 1998, Rough Sleeping
4 Social Exclusion Unit, July 1998, Rough Sleeping
5 Crisis, 2001, Trouble at Home
6 McVie, S. And Holmes, L., 2005, Family Functioning and Substance Use at Ages 12 to 17, Edinburgh Study of Youth Transitions and Crime report Number 9
7 The Centre for Social Justice, September 2008, The Next Generation; Duncan Smith, I. and Allen, G., 2008, Early Intervention: Good Parents, Great Kids, Better Citizens, The Centre for Social Justice and The Smith Institute
8 Olds D., 1997, 'The prenatal/early infancy project: Fifteen years later' in G.W.Albee & T.P. Gullotta, eds, Primary Prevention Works, Thousand Oaks, CA: Sage; Issues in Children's and Families' Lives, Vol VI
9 The Centre for Social Justice, January 2010, The Centre for Social Justice Green Paper on the Family; this paper suggests how such an approach could be implemented
10 The Centre for Social Justice, February 2009, Dying to Belong: An in-depth review of street gangs in Britain
11 The Centre for Social Justice, September 2009, Dynamic Benefits: Towards Welfare that Works

Hardest to Reach?

3. ON THE GROUND

Hilary Armstrong

*Services to help people with multiple needs and exclusions exist,
but only in limited geographical areas. How can government build
on its learning so far and expand the provision of services focused
on helping those most in need?*

In 21st century Britain, what can we do to change the life
chances of the most vulnerable of our society? These are
the people who end up in accident and emergency, or a
police cell, who are likely to be in and out of custody, who
may have an alcohol or drug addiction, and may well have
little or no contact with their families.

When I was Social Exclusion Minister in the Cabinet
Office, we took another look at people with multiple needs
and it was clear that they were often only accessing services in emergencies (the most expensive way), that no one
had overall responsibility for working with such vulnerable
adults, and that we spent a lot of money without significantly improving the lives of the people concerned. We set
up twelve pilots around the country called the Adults
Facing Chronic Exclusion pilots to see what could work
more effectively for this group, but also focused other work
on early intervention, to try to make sure that fewer people
end up in similar situations. Since I left government I have
had the privilege of working in the North East with The

Cyrenians – an organisation which works with the most excluded and vulnerable in many different ways. The Cyrenians have conducted one of the Adults Facing Chronic Exclusion (ACE) pilots which is now being mainstreamed in Newcastle. The service works with chronically excluded individuals who are not accessing existing services or who are deemed to be inappropriate for existing provision, often because of complex needs, and uses day and night outreach to seek out excluded individuals.

The unique feature of this pilot is that all the project workers are ex-service users who experienced chronic exclusion in the past. These are the people with whom the target group are most likely to engage, and they can be excellent role models. They have proved to be knowledge-able and passionate about the many indefinable barriers to accessing services, and they have empathy and insight into how to make contacts and initiate change. This is not an easy model, and The Cyrenians have had to keep a close eye on management and support for these workers. The Newcastle service helps individuals with multiple needs access specialist services, either by bringing these services directly to the excluded individuals, or by accompanying them to appointments to ensure that they actually attend, to advocate for them and jointly with these services to pro-mote the best outcome for the individual clients. So the project has helped individuals to significantly improve lev-els of engagement and inclusion but it has also had a wider effect, by influencing how local services are delivered so that they are better coordinated around the person in need, rather than operating within the rigid frameworks and eli-gibility criteria that so often act as barriers for those with chaotic lifestyles.

Another project where the Cyrenians work with the most vulnerable is the GAP project, which provides individual outreach and group support for women in Newcastle who are involved in sex work or are sexually exploited. The women have a wide spectrum of personal, social and economic needs which means that access to mainstream services presents real challenges for them. Again, what the Cyrenians call 'assertive outreach' is used to contact women wherever they feel comfortable, and they are frequently accompanied to appointments. The workers also try to provide alternative life experiences for the women, and have included sport and gym sessions with a personal trainer, creative writing, art, horse-riding and film making. There is also a weekly drop-in, run and organised by some of the women themselves.

Evaluation shows raised self esteem and a growing recognition among the women that they do have choices in their lives.

The unique feature of this pilot is that all the project workers are ex-service users who experienced chronic exclusion in the past.

Taking this work forward

What can we learn from this and other work, and what are the implications for progressive government? Clearly if we really want to tackle multiple needs, we cannot simply rely on those who are deeply excluded having the same formal rights as everyone else. Simply developing universal services does not, of itself, tackle inequality. The most vulnerable have complex needs, and expecting them to conform to the means by which mainstream services have traditionally been offered does not work. So what, then, should we be doing?

Firstly, services really do have to be reconfigured to ensure that they respond to the needs of the individual. We have been talking about personalisation and personal budgets for some time, but this is just part of the issue. It is also clear that there have to be more holistic ways of engaging and working with individuals, something that services often find incredibly difficult to do. That is where using the voluntary sector becomes even more important. It is in the voluntary sector that we see the flexibility and sensitivity to work in this more holistic way. Many of the ACE pilots are based, in different ways, around the provision of a 'consistent, trusted adult' to help first engage and then guide service users to the help they need. The key to success in such services is often the quality of the relationship that is developed between worker and service user. This requires true professionalism that has a large element of empathy. The successful projects also recognise the level of support that staff will need, particularly if the workforce is to include previous service users.

Secondly, it is clear that such holistic services will only work well if there is also a corresponding cultural shift across all other local services and agencies – statutory and voluntary. Holistic services like those described above in Newcastle rely on a wide range of mainstream partners to provide many of the interventions that individuals are being helped to access. All these partners must recognise the role that they have to play in tackling multiple needs, reducing barriers to accessing the services they provide, 'flexing' their eligibility criteria and providing a more personalised approach within their own individual specialisms.

All this means that commissioners are going to need to work in much more sensitive ways, where they agree across services on the outcomes they are looking for, and then offer contracts on that basis. If those contracts are over-prescriptive on process, they will be expensive and probably unsuccessful. It also means that we have to be more trusting of the voluntary sector directly delivering services, and not just see them as peripheral. Central government must also play a role in helping local commissioners to see the value of working in this way.

Making it happen
The work on multiple needs to date is providing clear evidence that the life chances of the most vulnerable who have complex needs can be transformed. Meeting a group of people with very complex needs last week, that was the most frequently used word - transformation - whether they were talking about their ability to control their addiction, their self-harm, their lack of self control and anger, or their relationship with their family.

We need to build on what we know works, widen its implementation across areas and ensure that central government has a clear focus on helping this group. There are hard lessons for us about public service reform, commissioning and how we work with individuals. We have a long way to go, but if we remain focused, it is clear that much can be achieved.

Hardest to Reach?

4. COST-EFFECTIVE, LOCAL AND PERSONAL

Alasdair Murray

Government efforts to reach people with the most complex needs have failed because they have missed people out, with many falling between the gaps or failing to engage with services. A liberal approach to helping adults with multiple needs must be more efficient and bespoke.

Since taking office in 1997, the Labour Government has made tackling social exclusion one of its key priorities. Alongside its anti-poverty targets, it has sought to try and tackle some of the most entrenched forms of social exclusion through public service agreements (PSAs) and the support of specialist cross-departmental bodies, like the Social Exclusion Unit.

However, this process has so far met with mixed success. By definition, the most socially excluded groups are the hardest to reach. These groups of people tend to have an array of complex needs, including substance abuse and mental health problems alongside periods of homelessness and regular brushes with prison and the probation system. They are the least able to engage effectively with services. They may require special provision, such as supported accommodation which is in short supply in many areas. Some are reluctant to change their lifestyle and resist support. A few are abusive or violent.

There is mounting evidence that the Government's well-intentioned policies are still failing to help those with the most complex needs. This has led to calls from groups, such as the Making Every Adult Matter (MEAM) coalition of charities, for the next Government to focus more closely on those who fall outside current policies.

This short essay argues that four key principles should inform the next Government's approach to dealing with the most intractable social exclusion problems.

First, government must improve its data on this group and its ability to measure progress.

Second, policy must be focused on achieving long term savings, by effective intervention to solve root causes – rather than constant and repeated spending on symptoms. Governments find such long term accounting difficult in normal economic conditions but with the pressing need to reduce overall spending accepted by all political parties, this becomes even more essential.

Third, government needs to build on local service delivery. Local service providers are by far the best placed to define precisely who is most in need of support and to work closely with the user to determine what help would be most effective. The Government is moving in this direction: the Total Place Initiative seeks to analyse the impact of all forms of public expenditure in a specific area, and should help to make spending more targeted and effective. However, the danger remains that the next Government will pay lip service to localism while keeping a close grip on the reins.

Finally, service provision must become more personal. It should be obvious that individuals who face an array of overlapping and complex problems will need specially tailored services. However, too often users complain they still face impersonal and inappropriate service delivery. Government should explore the possibility of giving service users greater control over the budget strings.

Data: what gets measured gets done

In 2007, the Government introduced Public Service Agreement 16 which was designed to tackle social exclusion among the most vulnerable adults. It sought to get the various agencies that are active in this field working together to increase the proportion of the most excluded in settled accommodation and in work, education or training. The Government chose to focus on four main groups: adult offenders under probation supervision; adults with moderate or worse learning difficulties; care leavers at the age of 19; and adults in contact with secondary mental health services.

Given the short period that the PSA has been in place, it is difficult to assess what difference has been made to outcomes, although the scale of the problem is now apparent. The most recent data, published in February 2010, shows that the number of people in contact with secondary mental health services and on the Care Programme Approach who are in 'settled accommodation' stood at 21.5 per cent, while employment rates stood at just 3.4 per cent.[1] The figures are better for those cases where there is full information: 60 per cent and 11 per cent respectively. Meanwhile, in 2008 the Government found that at the end of their license period, 77 per cent of offenders were in settled and suitable accommodation and 37 per cent of offenders were in employment.[2]

The danger is that the next Government will naturally seek to cut that which is most politically expedient.

Even if we accept their accuracy, these figures indicate the scale of the task for these groups. However, service providers closest to excluded people, believe that PSA 16 is failing to reach those who most need help.

There are three reasons for this. First, government has chosen to focus on groups it can relatively easily define and measure. This means that many individuals are simply missed. For example, an individual could have needs in a number of areas, which combined create a major challenge, but individually do not meet the threshold for intervention.

Second, an individual could be known to all the relevant services but not identified as a PSA client. Both point to the need for service providers, commissioners and government to define needs more broadly than those covered by the PSA 16, as suggested by the MEAM coalition.[3]

Third, those with the most complex needs are often reluctant to engage with services. While this may be choice – drug addiction keeps many from seeking help - stigma, perceived discrimination and low motivation are also important factors.

As outlined elsewhere in this book, the Making Every Adult Matter coalition has sought to make a rough estimate of how many people have multiple needs including those missing from the Government's current definition. In total there are around 140,000 people in prison or homeless. Of these, an estimated 40 per cent face multiple problems. There are thus 56,000 people across the country that have multiple needs and face exclusion. This might be an understatement, however, as other groups, like sex workers, may not be captured in these figures.

The next Government should expand the definition of the most excluded, while passing more powers to intervene simultaneously. It must then greatly improve the quality of data available.

Long term savings: the challenge of austerity

More accurate data will, of course, be vital to making the wider economic and social case for making better use of resources directed to the people who are the most difficult to reach. This will be even more essential in a context of public spending austerity, which looks set to dominate the next Parliament no matter which party forms the Government.

It is often the case that 'Cinderella' services such as mental health are easy targets for cuts during periods of fiscal consolidations. The danger is that the next Government will naturally seek to cut that which is most politically expedient. The repeated attempts of the main political parties to ring fence certain budgets only further increases the likelihood that less politically sensitive services will face the axe.

It is vital that the case for continued investment in services for those with multiple needs is made. This requires work clearly outlining the longer term costs to economy and society of sticking with the status quo, which far outweigh the spending necessary to provide effective services now. There is already evidence that effective drug treatment and homelessness services reduce public spending in the medium term. Drug users cost the Government more than £10,000 a year but every £1 spent on drug treatment saves a minimum of £9.50 in associated health and crime costs.[4]

The danger is that even if services for those with multiple needs are not directly targeted for cuts, they will suffer in any case as the Government makes a series of small 'salami' cuts across the board. Gus O'Donnell, the cabinet secretary, has suggested a useful alternative: establish 'single issue' budgets for cross-departmental spending areas such as social exclusion. It would ensure the Government would need to assess the overall impact of any spending reduction. It may also lead to further efficiencies by preventing people repeatedly 'recycling' through different parts of the criminal justice system, drug treatment, homelessness and mental health support.

The next Government should take the challenge of reducing the fiscal deficit as an opportunity to ask more profound questions about what it should and should not be funding and how money best reaches its intended targets. By any measure, it must remain a priority to provide suitable funding for those who are most excluded and face the hardest challenges in life. And in the medium term effective action now should yield savings in the future.

Local solutions

In many areas, the number of people with multiple needs will be relatively small. It is vital that these people are defined as locally as possible, although within the broad parameters set by national government in consultation with services users and providers from across the country.

Services also need to be delivered as locally as possible and make better use of the diversity of state and non-state organisations already working around social exclusion. This is in line with the trend in policy, as all the main parties are committed to some form of localism and greater diversity of provision. Here, the Government's Total Place Initiative (TPI) provides a useful way forward. The TPI requires all the various funding agencies to consider how they could better co-ordinate their funding streams in a particular area. Six out of the 13 pilot areas for the project have considered some aspect of social exclusion.

Personalised services

It is also vital that policymakers at all levels of government seek to accelerate the trend towards more personalised and user-led services. To be effective, services must be shaped by users, offer choice, avoid exclusions and build trust and confidence.

There is good evidence that users respond well to increased choice and responsibility. For example, the US 'Housing First' project seeks to get those with multiple needs into settled accommodation in mixed communities before completing other treatment.[5] Choice is an important element of the programme – users are able to decide on the apartment, furnishing, and the location and times of contact with support workers. From the outset, users are treated as capable of remaining stably housed despite their mental health and/or drug problems. The Housing First project in New York has recorded an 80 per cent retention rate over a two year period.

However, it is not yet the case that all UK services are tailoring provision to the needs of the individual. In particular, studies show that those with multiple needs face particular problems with the inflexibility of the benefits system and Job Centre Plus. One survey found that participants

It is vital that the case for continued investment in services for those with multiple needs is made.

with multiple needs experienced the Job Centre Plus to be "inefficient, impersonal and felt it often created barriers and exacerbated problems".[6]

To make services truly personal, people with multiple needs should be able to interact with one 'lead' provider. Service users are clear that they need to be seen regularly by one person who can help guide them through the system based on a single case history and not have to start from scratch in every new service. This opens up the possibility of "providing structured, focused support which enables people to set goals, gives structure to their lives and helps them develop problem solving skills".[7]

The Government has sought to establish support and clear guidelines for lead professionals.[8] These people take on responsibility for guiding people through the many different elements of the system. Leads include personal managers for those leaving care, offender managers for those in the probation system and care co-ordinators for mental health service users.

However, research has found a number of limitations to this system.[9] Lead professionals are often unaware of their own position. Many have heavy case loads which limit the time they can spend on services outside their specialism, and they sometimes lack the experience to ensure clients can find suitable accommodation. For their part, clients are sometimes unaware of who is acting as the lead professional. Lead professionals are also often unaware of PSA 16 and there is little evidence that they have adapted practices in light of it.

Instead of the current system, which imposes a default lead person who works at the first service the person uses, the lead professional should be independent of other key agencies. This would ensure they could offer impartial advice and champion the individual across the range of services.

The lead professional should also have access to a single budget for the service user enabling them to help make informed decisions about the best use of funds. This reform would require central government to remove barriers between different social exclusion budgets. It would open up the possibility of allowing users greater control over their budget and a move towards 'self-directed' care. This practice is now widespread in some of the services that those with multiple needs access. For example, mental health services users and those with learning disabilities already have control of parts of their budgets. The evidence to date is that, carefully managed, this can lead to improved outcomes and cost savings. It also offers an opportunity to work with the user to develop vital skills such as financial management, which are often lacking.

Conclusion – drawing in the hard to reach

The next Government has the opportunity to build on the work done over the last decade and create a policy approach that successfully engages with the hardest to reach in society. The looming spending constraints should not be an excuse for inaction. By any definition, helping those with multiple needs is a key function of public spending and should not be threatened by the current rethink about the role and scope of the state – however necessary this is. Nor should public sector austerity preclude further reform towards creating a flexible, responsible and personalised service structure for those with multiple needs. Such reform should bring savings. A cost-effective, local and personal approach offers real hope for those individuals facing the challenge of multiple needs.

Footnotes

1 http://www.cabinetoffice.gov.uk/social_exclusion_task_force/psa/indicators_data.aspx
2 http://www.hmg.gov.uk/linkuplinkin/home-job/offenders-probation.aspx
3 MEAM, 'A four point manifesto for tackling multiple needs and exclusions', September 2009
4 Godfrey et al, 'Economic analysis of costs and consequences of the treatment of drug misuse', Journal of Addiction 99 (6), 2004.
5 I Atherton and C McNaughton Nicholls, 'Housing First as a means of addressing multiple needs and homelessness', European Journal of Homelessness, Vol 2, December 2008.
6 Braithwaite, T., 'Multiple needs: service users' perspectives', Revolving Doors Agency, September 2009.
7 Braithwaite, T., 'Multiple needs: service users' perspectives', Revolving Doors Agency, September 2009.
8 Cabinet Office, 'Taking the lead: supporting the lead professional in tackling social exclusion', December 2009.
9 DCLG, 'PSA16 (socially excluded adults) qualitative research on settled accommodation, March 2010.

Hardest to Reach?

5. HOW TO JOIN UP GOVERNMENT

David Halpern and Akash Paun

For at least fifteen years, policy-makers have talked of the challenge of joining up government – ensuring that different arms of the state are acting in a co-ordinated, intelligent fashion. After a decade and a half of attempts to join up, government still struggles to work across boundaries. The results of this can be seen in the chaotic lives of people with multiple needs and exclusions, but there are many lessons to draw too.

"As one moved between the various departments it was obvious that, through the salaries of policemen, probation officers, social workers and so on, we were spending a fortune on a relatively focused section of the population... there had to be a more imaginative and effective way to use these resources."[1]

This quote could have been from yesterday. In fact it refers to a meeting of Permanent Secretaries – the heads of Whitehall departments – held in 1993. It's a sobering thought that, in many ways, little has changed. But we have made some progress. In particular, we have gained important insights into what drives exclusion and what works to get people out of it.

Political context

In the mid-1990's Peter Lilley raised the issue of government spending substantial sums on the same disadvantaged individuals in separate and ineffective silos. But it was the 1997 Labour administration who made it a central focus. It was the subject of

41

Blair's first major speech in government, and a new Social Exclusion Unit was created in the Cabinet Office.[2] Blair returned to the issue in 2006, reconstituting the Social Exclusion Task Force back into the Cabinet Office and handing the Cabinet Secretary – the head of the Civil Service – his only Public Service Agreement: social exclusion (PSA 16).[3]

The Conservative Party has also retained, or perhaps redis-covered, its interest in exclusion, arguing that problems such as family breakdown, welfare dependence, debt and addiction create "an ever-growing underclass" excluded from main-stream society.[4]

While government can claim to have made some progress over the past decade in reducing problems such as child pover-ty and the number of adults with no qualifications,[5] a critique levelled at government (not least by itself)[6] is that it has not suc-ceeded in tackling the "persistent and deep-seated exclusion of a small minority".[7] Adults with multiple needs are particularly likely to be 'left behind' as the complexity of their problems leaves them prone to 'falling into the gaps' between different support agencies, and to 'bouncing around the system', access-ing different services in an often 'chaotic' and expensive way. Such individuals can come to be seen as "everyone's problem but no one's particular responsibility".[8]

The scale of the problem
The Cabinet Office in 2007 estimated that 2 to 3 per cent of the population suffer from "deep and persistent exclusion".[9] The Making Every Adult Matter (MEAM) coalition has used a subset of this population in its definition of multiple needs and exclusions, focusing on individuals who are "routinely excluded from effective contact with the services they need" and "tend to live chaotic lives that are costly to society". As outlined earlier in this book, MEAM estimates that there are about 56,000 people fitting this definition in the prison and

homeless populations alone.[10] This figure excludes other high-cost, high-need people such as those living chaotic lifestyles in social and rented housing.

At the local level, adults with multiple problems are often well-known to services, councils and often to the public too, typically numbering around 100-300 in a large Local Authority area. Some areas have developed their own identification tools, such as the New Directions Team partnership in South London, whose shared assessment uses a range of behavioural indicators to assess whether particular individuals are suitable for referral to a programme of focused intervention.[11]

Other information comes from data collected under PSA 16. According to the latest reported data, there has been improvement on the indicators measuring accommodation rates for care leavers and ex-prisoners in probation (though

It is possible to identify those at high risk of multiple problems in adulthood from relatively early in childhood.

with wide variation across the country),[12] but stagnating or deteriorating rates of employment and education levels for these two groups.[13] For the other four indicators, relating to adults with learning disabilities and mental health problems, there is uncertainty about progress due to concerns with data quality.

The fiscal context: opportunity or threat?

Individuals with multiple needs and exclusions incur high costs for government through repetitive use of public services, a reliance on expensive emergency interventions (such as A&E), criminal justice responses, and welfare payments.

Individual case studies illustrate the high costs of multiple needs and exclusions. A simple estimate of direct annual expenditure on an 'average' adult with multiple needs in 2006 was around £23,000.[14] In many cases, it can be far more. For example, one individual, a former drug addict and serial offender, was estimated to have cost government in excess of £400,000 over several years in direct costs alone (not counting social costs of crime and anti-social behaviour).[15, 16]

On one hand, the need for government to cut the deficit should create a sharper focus on the high and often duplicated spend on adults with multiple needs. However, their relatively small numbers (including as voters), and the tendency of silo-based services to protect their core functions and cut collaborative and preventative measures in times of financial pressure are cause for real concern.

What works?

The 2006 social exclusion strategy showed that it was possible to identify those at high risk of multiple problems in adulthood from relatively early in childhood. For example, the 5 per cent most 'at-risk' 10-year-olds were found to be around 100 times more likely to be suffering from ten or more problems at the age of 30 than the 50 per cent of 10-year-olds at the lower end of the risk scale. The strategy identified a number of well-evidenced interventions for the early and teenage years, suggesting the possibility of long-term prevention, but it was much less confident about what works for adults.

Recently, the results for 12 pilot adult interventions have been released (see box on page 47). The results are very encouraging and despite the differing approaches of each pilot, suggest very similar conclusions. The majority of pilots led to marked improvements in the adults' lives as a whole. Substantial cost savings resulted, such as big reductions in the use of expensive emergency medical care and police call-outs. And there was a simple common thread in the successful pilots – the introduction of a consistent trusted adult – at a relatively modest cost of around £10-20 per hour.[17] Government should now seek to build on the learning from these pilots to support future policy development and further implementation of similar schemes.

Removing the barriers to joined-up working
While over 80 per cent of senior civil servants in a recent Institute for Government survey believed Whitehall had made significant improvements in joining-up over the past five years, nearly 60 per cent believed that government remained a long way from where it should be in this regard.[18] National approaches to address joining-up have included: joint strategies, specialist units, cross-cutting Ministers, cross-cutting targets such as those in PSA 16, and valuing collaboration in promotions and Capability Reviews. However, ownership of the multiple needs issue across government remains unclear and fragmented.

Fragmentation in Whitehall can also cascade down to the local level with detrimental effect.[19] Frontline practitioners report that multi-agency working is hampered by factors including:

- Differing and sometimes contradictory target regimes;
- Silo-like commissioning structures that do not focus on multiple needs;
- Restricted budgetary flexibility and difficulty in seeing cost efficiencies across separate budgets.

Added to this are the issues faced by all agencies in local areas of culture, funding, staffing and the day-to-day challenges of working with a complex client group, Attempts to address local joining up have included the encouragement of multi-agency working through the revamped Local Area Agreement framework, strengthening the 'place leadership' role of Local Strategic Partnerships, and a reduced plethora of central targets. Assessing areas as a whole, such as via the new Comprehensive Area Assessments, are also an important part of the story.

At the individual level, the key ingredient for making change happen seems to be a lead practitioner – a trusted consistent person who comes to understand the individual in a rounded way, cares about them, and gets them the help that they need.

In many areas this kind of practical coordination is much needed. As one recent study of poor families in Sheffield showed, there often remains a bewildering complexity of different teams and services, constrained by local, regional and national targets and reporting to different central departments, the local Jobcentre Plus and the government regional office.[20] Too regularly, coordination between local agencies remains poor and no-one in the area has a strategic oversight for people with multiple needs and exclusions.

Many have concluded that the weak link is money. Budgets split into discrete pots for specialist agencies at both national and local level, especially when reinforced by separate accountability agencies, make silos hard to break. As one interviewee complained "If you split money and governance like that you almost neuter the project before it starts, it proves very difficult to do and you are almost doing it on good will." This suggests a role for dedicated budgets for cross-cutting priorities (eg with 'joint key' arrangements for release). The pooling of budgets at a local level, as being explored in the Total Place initiative, is also promising. Interestingly, the results of the adult pilots suggest that, at the individual level, complete pooling of resources into individual budgets may not be necessary to get better outcomes, though some cash to help with tailored solutions can be helpful.

Conclusion

The new Government formed after May 2010, whichever party or parties it comprises, will be under great pressure to bring the fiscal deficit down. There is a real danger that the strong silo-based character of British government, from Whitehall to the front line, will lead to innovative and cross-cutting programs for adults with multiple problems being cut in order to protect conventional mainstream services. Those working to improve the lives of these adults will need to buttress their moral and compassionate arguments with robust cost-benefit analyses. In this respect, the recent and positive results of the ACE pilots are likely to be critical.

Adults facing Chronic Exclusion (ACE) Pilot Projects
In 2006 the Government launched a set of pilot projects, with 12 local areas given funding totalling £6m to trial and evaluate innovative methods of improving outcomes for adults with complex needs.[21] Sponsored by four government departments,[22] the ACE pilots have focussed on three main areas:

- "System change – simplifying the complexities associated with several statutory services working collaboratively (e.g. housing, social care, benefits, health and criminal justice system) to offer co-ordinated support to someone with multiple needs.
- Transition points – helping people to negotiate difficult times in their lives such as leaving prison, leaving care and fleeing domestic violence.
- System navigation – Offering practical help to people to access several services at one time."[23]

Preliminary (unpublished) findings of the ACE pilot projects suggest that a relatively low investment of around £50 per month per client led to behavioural changes that delivered cash benefits. For instance, clients of the projects were found to have reduced their use of expensive emergency treatments and instead doubled their use of GP visits at a tenth of the cost. More data is due to be published shortly.

Footnotes

1 Sir Michael Partridge, quoted in Halpern (1998) in Oppenheim, C (ed) An inclusive society: strategies for tackling poverty, p 270

2 Mulgan, G in Oppenheim, C (ed), pp259-268

3 See Cabinet Office 2007. PSA Delivery Agreement 16, at: http://tinyurl.com/yz6jopo

4 Centre for Social Justice 2006. Breakdown Britain: Interim report on the state of the nation, p.13. At: http://www.centreforsocialjustice.org.uk/client/downloads/CSJ%20FINAL%20(2).pdf

5 The number of children in absolute poverty fell by 1.7m to 1.7m between 1998/99 and 2007/08 while the number in relative poverty fell by 500,000 to 2.9m. However, progress in this area has slowed if not stalled as a result of the recession. Source: HM Treasury, Autumn Performance Report 2009, p.67. The proportion of working-age adults with no qualifications has fallen from 18 per cent in 1998 to 12 per cent in 2008. However, it is suggested that this is primarily due to the retirement of older unskilled people. Source: The Poverty Site, 'Working-age adults without qualifications', at: http://www.poverty.org.uk/59/index.shtml, accessed on 5 March 2010.

6 Cabinet Office 2006. Reaching Out: An Action Plan on Social Exclusion, at: http://tinyurl.com/5sorzn

7 Cabinet Office 2006. Reaching Out, p.8.

8 CESU, 2007. Service responses, and outcomes for adults described as having chaotic lives and multiple needs. A scoping exercise, p.24. At: http://tinyurl.com/ylxvew2

9 Cabinet Office 2007. Reaching Out: Progress on Social Exclusion, p.5. At: http://tinyurl.com/yjmhh9x

10 Making Every Adult Matter 2009. A four-point manifesto for tackling multiple needs and exclusions, p.8. At: http://www.meam.org.uk/wp-content/uploads/2009/09/MEAM-report.pdf

11 Cabinet Office 2009. New Directions Team, South West London. At: http://www.cabinetoffice.gov.uk/social_exclusion_task_force/adults/new_directions.aspx

12 For instance, in some areas, over 90 per cent of "care leavers at age 19" are in settled accommodation as opposed to just 59 per cent in the worst performing area. Source: Institute for Government analysis of data downloaded from: Communities and Local Government, Floor Targets Interactive, at: http://www.fti.communities.gov.uk/DataDownload.aspx, accessed 22 February 2010.

13 Specifically: 'Offenders under probation supervision in settled and suitable accommodation', rose from 76.5 per cent to 78.5 per cent in the past year; 'Care leavers at age 19 in suitable accommodation' rose from 88.4 per cent to 89.6 per cent in the past two years; 'Offenders under probation supervision in employment' fell to 46.4 per cent; and 'Care leavers at age 19 in employment' fell back to its 2007 baseline level of 63 per cent. Source: Cabinet Office 2009. Autumn Performance Report, pp.20-21. At: http://www.cabinetoffice.gov.uk/media/319667/apr2009.pdf In general, while employment rates rose in almost every category over the last decade, the big exception was those with no qualifications for whom employment rates fell.

14 David Halpern, Social exclusion: bringing opportunity for all, Presentation at Chequers, 29th August, 2006.

15 This figure included £152k in policing, court and prison costs; £40k in hospital visits and drug treatment; £178k in accommodation and support; and £37k on outreach. Source: Making Every Adult Matter 2009. A four-point manifesto, p.22.

16 Macro-spending estimates tend to be even larger. For instance, Class A drug use alone has been estimated to cost £13.9 billion per year in terms of increased rates of crime alone. Singleton, N., Murray, R., and Tinsley, L. 2004–05. Measuring Different Aspects of Problem Drug Use: Methodological developments. Home Office Online Report 16/06, p.41.

17 Source: Unpublished findings of Adults facing Chronic Exclusion (ACE) Pilot projects, presented by Nick O'Shea at the Institute for Government on 25 February 2010.

18 See Simon Parker, Akash Paun, Jonathan McClory and Kate Blatchford 2010. Shaping Up: A Whitehall for the Future (London: Institute for Government), in particular chapter 4.

19 Clinical Effectiveness Support Unit 2007. Service responses, and outcomes for adults described as having chaotic lives and multiple needs. p.19.

20 See: Sheffield City Council (2009) Developing the Whole Household Model. (Sheffield City Council: unpublished paper)

21 More information at: http://www.cabinetoffice.gov.uk/social_exclusion_task_force/adults.aspx

22 Home Office, Communities and Local Government, Department of Health, Department for Work and Pensions.

23 Cabinet Office, About the ACE Programme, at: http://www.cabinetoffice.gov.uk/social_exclusion_task_force/adults/about_ace.aspx, accessed 18 Feb 2010.

Hardest to Reach?

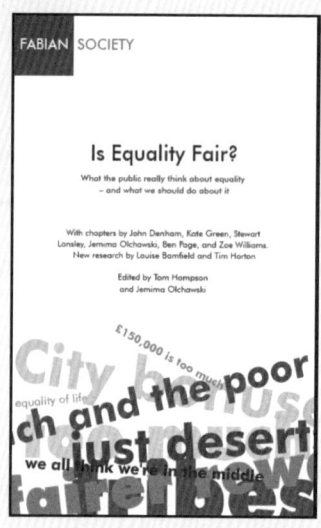

Is Equality Fair?

What the public really think about equality – and what we should do about it.

Edited by Tom Hampson and Jemima Olchawski

In this Fabian Special, John Denham, Kate Green, Stewart Lansley, Jemima Olchawski, Ben Page and Zoe Williams respond to new Fabian work on public attitudes to fairness.

The work, commissioned by the Joseph Rowntree Foundation, found that most people think that 'deserved' inequalities are fair, and attitudes towards those on low incomes were often more negative than attitudes towards the rich. However, we also found that people strongly support progressive tax and benefits.

"If we ever give up on fairness and equality the centre left will have lost all meaning. The Fabian research on voter attitudes doesn't tell us to give up; it just asks us to think about how we move forward." – John Denham MP

The Solidarity Society

Why we can afford to end poverty, and how to do it with public support.

Tim Horton and James Gregory

This report sets out a strategy for how to reduce, eliminate and prevent poverty in Britain.

'The Solidarity Society' is the final report of a project to commemorate the centenary of Beatrice Webb's 1909 Minority Report of the Royal Commission on the Poor Law. It addresses how the values and insights of the Minority Report can animate and inspire a radical contemporary vision to fight and prevent poverty in modern Britain.

The report makes immediate proposals to help build momentum for deeper change. It also seeks to learn lessons from the successes and failures of post-war welfare history, as well as from international evidence on poverty prevention.

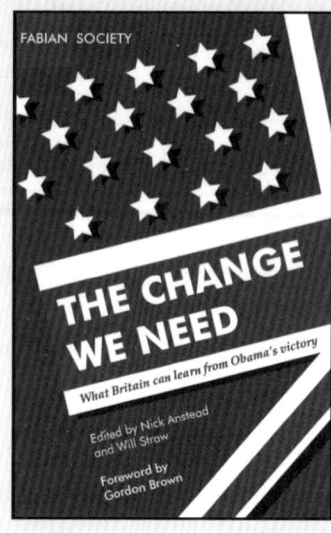

The Change We Need

What Britain can learn from Obama's victory

Edited by Nick Anstead and Will Straw, with a forward by Gordon Brown

How can a party in office for more than a decade recapture its idealism? Can Labour hope to draw on the same popular enthusiasm that swept Barack Obama to victory?

In 'The Change We Need', staffers from the Obama campaign come together with senior British and American politicians, academics, thinkers and campaigners to draw forwardlooking and optimistic lessons for the British progressive left.

Together they show that the opportunity can only be seized if we fundamentally rethink the ways we do politics in Britain, by rejecting the command-and-control model of the New Labour era and energising grassroots supporters.

"Contained within these pages are the ideas of tomorrow – the new ways of working that will help Labour members do even more to change our world." – Gordon Brown